W9-BLV-625

Blockade Runners and Ironclads

Blockade Runners and Ironclads

Naval Action in the Civil War

by Wallace B. Black

A First Book

Franklin Watts
A Division of Grolier Publishing
New York - London - Hong Kong - Sydney
Danbury, Connecticut

Photos ©: Photographs ©: Archive Photos: cover, 25, 34; Art Resource/Museum of the City of New York: 37; Corbis-Bettmann: 6, 14,15, 18, 21, 23, 32, 45, 46, 50, 52; George Eastman House: 43; The Museum of the Confederacy, Richmond, Virginia: 48 (Katherine Wetzel), 10; North Wind Picture Archives: 8, 12, 17; Stock Montage, Inc.: 27, 30, 39, 40, 49; Stock Montage, Inc.: 56.
Map by Accurate Art, Inc.: 29.

Library of Congress Cataloging-in-Publication Data

Black, Wallace B.
Blockade runners and ironclads: naval action in the Civil War/ by Wallace B. Black
p.   cm.—(A First book)
Includes bibliographical references and index.
Summary: Discusses Civil War naval battles, ships, and the struggle for control of
    crucial waterways, demonstrating how the Northern side was able to build up
    its navy and eventually blockade the Southern ports.
ISBN 0–531–20272–0
1. United States—History—Civil War, 1861–1865—Naval operations—Juvenile liter-
    ature. 2.   United States—History—Civil War, 1861–1865—Blockades—Juvenile
    literature. 3.   Armored vessels—United States—History—19th century—
    Juvenile literature. [1. United States—History—Civil War, 1861–1865—Naval
    operations. 2. United States. Navy—History.] I. Black, Wallace B. II. Title.
    III. Series.
E591.B56   1997
973.7'5—dc20

96–31643
CIP
AC

CONTENTS

Chapter One
THE WAR BEGINS

Cotton was shipped from the busy port at Charleston, South Carolina.

At 4:30 A.M. on April 12, 1861, the soldiers of the South fired their first shots against Fort Sumter in the harbor of Charleston, South Carolina. The North surrendered Fort Sumter the next day. Within weeks, President Abraham Lincoln called for 75,000 volunteers to serve in the Union army. He wanted these troops to put down the "insurrection" of the eleven southern states that had seceded, or withdrawn, from the Union. The War Between the States had begun.

Lincoln also wanted to expand the United States Navy. He wanted enough ships and sailors to be able to blockade all southern ports so that southern ships could neither enter nor leave. Meanwhile, the Confederate States of America—a new nation made up of those states that seceded—began to pull together an army of 400,000 volunteers.

A DIFFERENT NORTH AND SOUTH

In 1861, the northern states had about 19 million people. The South had only 9 million, including about 3.5 million slaves. The northern states already had a lot of industry. New York State alone contained more factories than all southern states put together.

The North owned thousands of ships. For generations, seafarers and shipbuilders had lived in the New England states and had sailed the oceans of the world. The North was able to create a strong navy very quickly. The South was not.

The seamen of the northeastern states had numerous ships when the Civil War started. This is the harbor at Boston, Massachusetts.

Southern states had concentrated on growing cotton. They had to be able to ship this cotton to England in order to get the money to buy weapons. The seceding states armed a few merchant vessels. They also purchased warships from Great Britain that could capture Union ships on the Atlantic Ocean. They began to build fighting ships, too, especially fast ships that could slip past blockaders.

The Southerners also planned to build warships that

were covered, or clad, in iron. They hoped these "iron-clads" could ram into and crush the wooden hulls of Union ships. However, the South did not have all the materials, factories, and skilled shipbuilders they needed to put up a good fight at sea.

THE UNION NAVY GROWS

The United States Navy was very strong in the War of 1812, but by 1860 it had become weak. Only about nine thousand officers and sailors were on active duty. Many of those officers were Southerners who resigned to join the new Confederate navy. The Union navy needed more people.

The Union navy had forty-two vessels in active service, and only twelve of those were really modern warships. The rest were older sailing craft. To rebuild its navy quickly, the Union planned to convert hundreds of merchant vessels into warships. About 130 existing ships of all types were purchased, armed, and sent south to blockade southern ports. New England shipyards were then ordered to build fifty-two new warships in ninety days. Like the South, the North began to develop ironclads.

Chapter Two
BLOCKADE! THE ANACONDA PLAN

The Union planned to blockade all southern ports. They thought this would prevent the South from shipping cotton, its main resource. The South would also be unable to receive weapons and other supplies from foreign

The CSS Armstrong *was typical of ships that could be propelled either by wind or engine power.*

countries. The Union called the blockade the "Anaconda Plan," named after the giant snake that squeezes its prey to death. They hoped the blockade would squeeze the Confederacy into submission and force it to surrender.

The Anaconda Plan also called for taking control of the Mississippi River. That would cut off supplies and communications between the western states of Texas and Arkansas and the eastern Confederate states.

The plan wasn't going to be easy to carry out. The coastline of the Confederate states was more than 3,500 miles (5,630 km) long, stretching from Virginia to the Gulf of Mexico. Union ships could not block all the ports. They focused on six major ports, but Confederate blockade runners managed to slip out. Throughout the war, they got past Union patrols about five thousand times, but that was not enough to move all the cotton out and supplies in. During the war, more than 1,500 blockade runners were captured by the Union navy.

THE CAPE HATTERAS RAID

The South won the first major battle, Bull Run (also called Manassas), in July 1861. The stunned North needed a victory, and they looked to the navy for it.

Within weeks, the Union put together its first fleet. Their first target would be the Hatteras Inlet, a major southern port in North Carolina. The fleet was small but had considerable firepower, and it was accompanied by boats filled with armed soldiers. The goal was to capture Fort Hatteras and nearby Fort Clark, on Pamlico Sound.

The fleet set sail from the channel called Hampton

Ships of four different Union squadrons patrolled the major ports along the Atlantic and Gulf of Mexico coasts. They succeeded in blockading the movement of most arms and other goods in and out of the South.

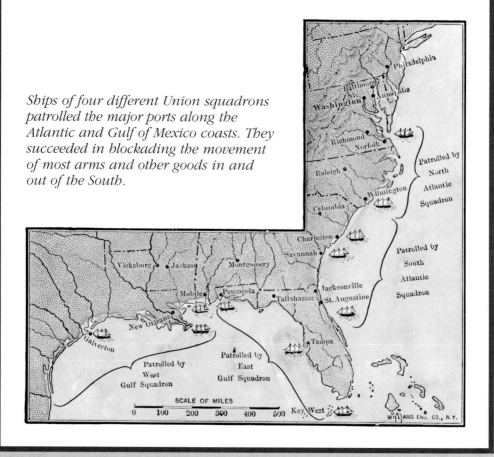

Roads in Virginia on August 27, 1861. Major General Benjamin F. Butler was in command of about eight hundred ground troops that were to land at Cape Hatteras.

The Union warships attacked the two nearby forts with heavy gunfire, and the USS *Monticello* headed into Pamlico Sound. Both forts immediately fired on it. But the *Monticello,* backed by the *Minnesota, Wabash,* and *Susquehanna,* was able to land the first Union troops.

Although Fort Hatteras had been reinforced during the night, the Confederates could not stop the invading Union troops. They ran up the white flag, surrendering the two forts.

This victory gave the Union control of the main passage into North Carolina. This first amphibious operation—one using both ground and naval forces—was a complete success, and it raised the spirits of the people in the North.

THE SOUTH ATLANTIC BLOCKADING SQUADRON

Commodore Samuel Francis Du Pont, a veteran of the Mexican War, received orders from Secretary of the Navy Gideon Welles to create a South Atlantic Blockading Squadron. This squadron, along with the army, was to

Samuel Francis Du Pont helped organize the Anaconda Plan and then took command of the South Atlantic Blockading Squadron to control South Carolina ports.

invade the ports and beaches of South Carolina.

Du Pont assembled a fleet of fifty ships in three months. In September 1861, they headed for Port Royal, South Carolina. The stronger ships entered the port on November 7 and moved back and forth, bombarding Fort Beauregard on the east and Fort Walker on the west. The forts surrendered after only two days of battle. The Union navy had another victory and control of two more major Confederate seaports.

The Anaconda Plan was working.

Chapter Three
The Monitor and the Merrimack

O n March 9, 1862, President Lincoln and his cabinet were in special session. They had just received the news that a brand-new Confederate ironclad, the CSS *Virginia,* had successfully attacked and sunk the USS *Congress* and the USS *Cumberland,* two of the largest warships in the Union navy. The new enemy warship

Abraham Lincoln's Secretary of the Navy, Gideon Welles, introduced ironclads to the United States Navy.

had come down the James River from Norfolk Navy Yard and into Hampton Roads, the huge bay where the large Union fleet was anchored.

The cabinet members did not know anything about the new Confederate ship. They thought it might come up the Potomac River and bombard Washington, D.C., or head out to sea to attack and sink other Union vessels at will.

Everyone was panic-stricken except Secretary of the Navy Gideon Welles. He knew that an equally fearsome Union ironclad, the USS *Monitor*, was on its way to Hampton Roads from New York. It would be there that very night.

THE MERRIMACK

Both the North and South knew about ironclad ships from France and Britain. When the war started, they decided to build similar ships. The *Virginia* had actually started as a Union warship, called the *Merrimack*. It was docked in Norfolk when the Confederates took over the navy yard. Rather than surrender their ship, Union sailors set fire to it, and it burned to the waterline. The Confederates did not have the time or resources to build an ironclad from scratch, so they built on the hull

The United States frigate Merrimack, *before (left) and after (below) its conversion by the South into the ironclad* Virginia

of the *Merrimack* instead. They renamed the ship the CSS *Virginia,* but many people, even the Southerners, continued to call it the *Merrimack.*

The new ship was awesome. It was 273 feet (83.2 m) long, covered by 800 tons of iron plate, and it carried twelve guns, 330 men, and huge steam engines. But it was also top-heavy, making it hard to maneuver. It could not move in water less than 22 feet (6.7 m) deep, and its engines were not nearly powerful enough to propel its weight.

In February 1862, the *Merrimack* prepared to attack the Union blockade squadron stationed in Hampton

The CSS Merrimack *(right) sank the USS* Cumberland *before its confrontation with the* Monitor.

Roads. It boldly entered the channel, where the Union fleet fired on it. Union soldiers were stunned as they watched their cannonballs bounce off the ship's grease-coated metal sides.

The *Merrimack* attacked and sank the USS *Cumberland* by ramming into the wooden hull. It then turned toward the USS *Congress.* The sailors of the *Congress* ran their ship into shallow water where the *Merrimack* could not follow. That defiant gesture, though, left the ship at the *Merrimack*'s mercy.

The *Merrimack's* captain, Commodore Franklin Buchanan, bombarded the *Congress* and then rescued its crew. When Union batteries continued to fire on the rescuers, Buchanan was wounded, and he ordered the *Merrimack* to back off. Then his men fired red-hot cannonballs at the *Congress,* setting it on fire.

With night coming on, the Union ships sailed into shallow water where Buchanan could not reach them. He took the *Merrimack* back upriver to repair its ram, prow, and smokestack. He planned to return and attack the Union fleet again in the morning.

THE MONITOR

Union naval engineers had reviewed many designs for ironclads before accepting one by John Ericsson. Ericsson's creation, the *Monitor,* was a strange-looking ship. It was completely clad in iron and had a single revolving gun turret on a flat deck. Some called it a "self-propelling gun platform." Others ridiculed it, calling it "a cheesebox on a raft."

The Union navy launched the *Monitor* in late January 1862 and sent it down the coast on February 25. The ship, 172 feet (53 m) long, held a crew of nine officers and forty-seven sailors, commanded by Lieutenant John Worden. Informed by telegraph of the situation with the *Merrimack*, Worden set out on March 6 to Hampton Roads to challenge the Confederate ship.

THE BATTLE OF THE IRONCLADS

Commander Buchanan was seriously wounded, so Lieutenant Catesby Jones was in command of the *Merrimack*. On March 9, early in the morning, he was preparing to attack the grounded USS *Minnesota* when the *Monitor* suddenly pulled out from behind the huge Union warship. Jones and his men watched wide-eyed as the odd craft moved out to meet their attack.

The Confederate warship fired. It was still far from the *Minnesota*. Lieutenant Worden ordered the *Monitor* to return fire.

The two ships battled for six hours. The faster and more maneuverable *Monitor* was able to avoid being hit by the larger ship. It fired steadily and began to do serious damage to the *Merrimack*. A lucky shot from the *Merrimack* struck the *Monitor*'s pilot house, temporarily blinding Worden. Lieutenant Samuel Greene moved the *Monitor* into shallow water so that he could tend to

The CSS Merrimack *(center) was crippled by the northern ironclad,* Monitor *(bottom), in the Battle of Hampton Roads, the first battle between iron ships in the Civil War.*

Worden's wounds and prepare for further battle.

Thinking the Union vessel was retreating, Lieutenant Jones of the *Merrimack* decided to return up the James River to the base at Norfolk. He was afraid his ship could not stand much more punishment.

The battle, technically a draw, was actually a victory for the North. The *Monitor* was ready to continue battle the next day. The *Merrimack*, though, was seriously damaged and would never fight again. Two months later, when the Confederates had to abandon Norfolk, the *Merrimack* was burned to keep it out of the hands of the Union navy. However, during the course of the Civil War, the South would eventually build twenty-two ironclad ships.

Pleased with the *Monitor's* performance in Hampton Roads, the Union navy soon had many more ironclads in production. They called them all "monitors" after the original northern ironclad ship. The Union navy was growing. It would soon be able to wage battles in many places at once. One of the most important would be the Mississippi River.

Chapter Four
THE MISSISSIPPI CAMPAIGN

O n May 26, 1861, the Union began its campaign to conquer New Orleans and gain control of the Mississippi River, thus cutting the Confederacy in two. The USS *Brooklyn* took up position in the Gulf of Mexico

The CSS Manassas, *first ironclad on the Mississippi*

off the mouth of the Mississippi to stop blockade runners trying to escape to sea from port. Within a week, it captured its first two merchant vessels carrying goods from Europe to the Confederates.

The Union blockaders had less success in stopping blockade runners that were trying to reach the sea. The Mississippi River has four outlets to the sea, so it was difficult for the blockaders to watch all routes. One Confederate ship, the CSS *Sumter,* sneaked past the blockade on June 30. The Union would later pay dearly for letting it escape.

IRONCLADS ON THE MISSISSIPPI

Soon after the war began, the Confederate navy began construction of the *Manassas.* It was to be an ironclad ram as well as a seagoing tugboat. Several other vessels were also converted into ironclad rams.

On October 11, 1861, the partially ironclad *Manassas* went into action, the first ironclad on the Mississippi. Its main armament was a large rifle cannon—the bore had spiral grooves that gave fired projectiles greater range and accuracy. The ship quickly attacked four Union blockaders on the lower river. Driving at full speed, the

POOK'S TURTLES

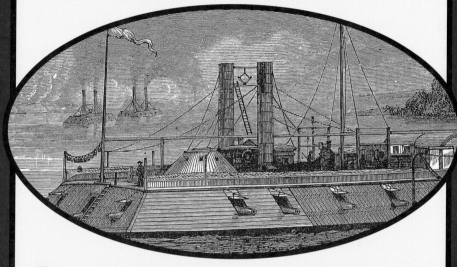

In St. Louis, Missouri, millionaire engineer and riverman James B. Eads was given a contract to build seven ironclads. The ships, designed by Samuel Pook, were nicknamed "Pook's Turtles" because of their humped shape. Eads, who had built the first metal bridge over the Mississippi River, also converted two large riverboats into gunboats by adding armor and guns. Almost twice the size of the ironclads, they were the most formidable warships on the river.

These nine boats, along with about forty other gunboats, made up the Union's Western Flotilla on the Mississippi. The river fleet was based at Cairo, Illinois.

Manassas rammed the USS *Richmond,* forcing it to run aground to keep from sinking.

Far to the north, where the Mississippi and Ohio Rivers meet, a major campaign began. Under the command of army general Ulysses S. Grant and Commodore Andrew Foote, the Union was planning to move its troops down the Mississippi and other rivers.

River warfare began in November 1861, when Grant's army and some gunboats commanded by Henry Walke attacked Confederate forces at Belmont, Missouri. The Union troops came up against a strong Confederate force and returned north to Cairo, Illinois.

FORT HENRY AND FORT DONELSON

In February 1862, Grant was ready to move south again. He controlled not just the Mississippi and Ohio Rivers, but also the Tennessee and Cumberland Rivers where they entered the Ohio River east of Cairo. Two Confederate forts, Henry and Donelson, guarded these two rivers, the gateway to the Deep South.

Grant advanced overland. Aided by Foote's ironclads on the river, he captured Fort Henry on the Tennessee River but found that most of the Confederate soldiers

An explosion of a gun aboard the USS Carondelet, *one of Pook's Turtles, during the attack on Fort Donelson*

had abandoned the fort. The Confederates marched overland to Fort Donelson, 10 miles (16 km) west on high ground over the Cumberland. Grant's men pursued them.

Commodore Foote and his gunboats returned to the Ohio River and then moved down the Cumberland. They planned to bombard the Confederates at Fort Donelson into submission. But this would not be easy. The Confederate troops at Fort Donelson held strong and damaged the Union ships below with cannon fire.

Grant and his ground forces attacked Fort Donelson from the rear. The Confederates decided they could no longer defend the fort. They tried to drive Grant's men away long enough to escape. But they failed to get away, and they had to return to the fort to surrender.

The Union now had complete control of the two rivers and could use them to pursue the Confederates. After repairing damage to his fleet, Commodore Foote headed south on the Mississippi, while Grant's army moved south along the Tennessee and Cumberland Rivers. At the same time, the Union Army of the Mississippi—18,000 troops, led by General John Pope— moved south on the Missouri side of the river to attack New Madrid, Missouri.

BATTLE FOR ISLAND NUMBER 10

The islands of the Mississippi were known by numbers rather than names. Island Number 10, south of Cairo, was heavily fortified by the Confederates. They also had a major force at New Madrid, Missouri, and strong batteries on the Tennessee shore across from Island 10.

The southern defenses were so strong that Commodore Foote would not attempt a naval attack.

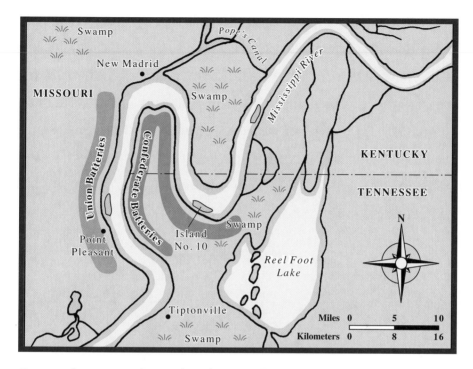

General Pope, though, demanded that Foote attack and get past Island Number 10. The Union fleet bombarded the island and the nearby shore installations, but it could not make its way past.

Pope, meanwhile, wanted to avoid a long march inland through swamps. So he had his army dig a long canal from a point above Island 10 through heavy wetlands along the Missouri shore. The troops moved along this canal on barges. Then they bombarded southern forces at New Madrid with heavy artillery.

Commodore Foote, who had been wounded at Fort Donelson, turned command over to Captain Henry Walke. Walke reinforced the ironclad USS *Carondelet,* and, in the dark of night during a storm, let it float past Island 10. The Confederates opened fire with every gun they had. But they could not see through the darkness and rain, so only a few shots struck the Union ironclad as it cruised safely past.

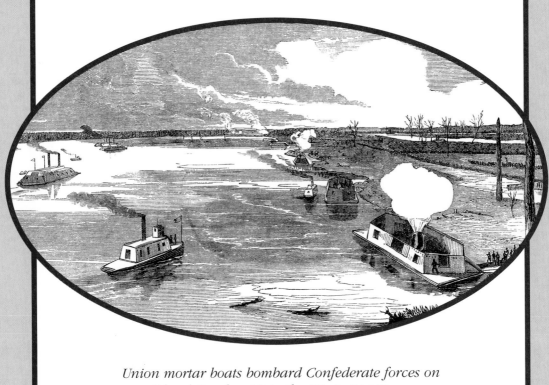

Union mortar boats bombard Confederate forces on Island Number 10 in the Mississippi River.

Two more ironclads also got past the island. Captain Walke's fleet joined General Pope's troops and attacked Point Pleasant, Tennessee. Walke assured Pope that it was now safe for him to cross the river into Tennessee.

Inland, along the Tennessee River, Grant was moving steadily south, supported by naval gunboats. The mighty Battle of Shiloh was about to begin in Tennessee. Although that battle turned into one of the bloodiest of the war, it was at best a draw. But without the navy gunboats, the Union might have been defeated.

THE CONFEDERATES FIGHT BACK

Union gunboats sailing south from New Madrid began to bombard Fort Randolph and Fort Pillow on the Tennessee River. Every day in May 1862, gunboats lofted mortar shells against the Confederate fortifications.

One foggy morning, the routine was suddenly broken. Confederate vessels steamed through the mist. They headed directly for the ironclad USS *Cincinnati,* which was tethered to the riverbank.

These Confederate gunboats were a new kind of river craft. Each boat had a long, sharp metal beam attached to its bow. Such a vessel, moving at full speed, could ram an enemy ship and drive a hole into its hull.

The *Cincinnati* quickly cut loose, but it was too late. One of the new boats, the *General Bragg,* drove its ram deep into the *Cincinnati*. The *Cincinnati* began to pull free, and its cannons blasted the *General Bragg* broadside, putting it out of the fight.

Several more Confederate ships came out and rammed the *Cincinnati*. They also hit the Union ironclad *Mound City* and drove it into shallow water.

The Union river fleet included many different kinds of ships.

The Confederate commander, seeing more Union ironclads steaming toward him, turned back south, delighted with the success of his new ships. Their presence stopped the Union from taking the forts before southern soldiers had to abandon them.

UNION RAMS

An engineer named Charles Ellet, Jr., built a small fleet of Union rams. He did the work within forty days and arrived at Fort Pillow soon after the Confederate victory. But Union land forces had already captured the fort. Ellet then went to Fort Randolph and found that the Confederates had abandoned it. The way south on the Mississippi was clear all the way to Memphis, Tennessee.

The unfortified city of Memphis was protected by a fleet of Confederate rams led by Captain James Montgomery. At dawn on June 6, 1862, residents of Memphis went to the river to watch them prepare for battle. Suddenly the Union ram *Queen of the West,* leading several others, steamed up to meet the enemy.

The first contact was between the *Queen of the West* and a Confederate ram, the *Colonel Lovell.* At first it appeared that the two rams would collide head-on, but

The gundeck of a Mississippi gunboat is quiet here, but it would be the scene of noisy action during the battle to take Fort Henry.

the *Lovell* lost power in one engine and swung sideways. It received a terrible blow from the *Queen* and began to sink. Then the ram *General Sumter* plowed into the *Queen* and disabled it. A second Union ram, the *Monarch,* attacked and rammed the CSS *Beauregard.*

By this time, the large Union ironclads had arrived. The remaining Confederate rams, outnumbered and outgunned, fled south. Union ships destroyed or grounded them one by one. Only one Confederate ram escaped.

The victorious Union naval forces returned to

Memphis and sent a small force ashore to raise the Stars and Stripes over the city. Strangely, the only Union sailor to die as a result of the battle was the builder of the rams, Charles Ellet, Jr.

THE CAPTURE OF NEW ORLEANS

Union leaders knew that capturing New Orleans would be a serious blow to the Confederates. They decided to launch a major attack on the city. Union naval commander David Farragut received orders to move up the river from the Gulf of Mexico and capture the city.

Farragut would have to pass two Confederate forts, Jackson and St. Philip, about 25 miles (40 km) north of the Gulf along the river. Both forts were strong and had tremendous firepower. He would also have to get past a line of dead ship hulls anchored in the main channel of the river to block incoming vessels.

Commander David Dixon Porter, Farragut's foster brother, led a small fleet of vessels carrying heavy mortar cannons. He hoped his ships could bombard the two forts into submission, but even after six days of heavy shelling the forts held firm. Farragut made a bold plan. He sent two small gunboats out to slip past the forts under cover of a moonless night. They cut loose the sunken hulls, which drifted out of the way. Then, at two o'clock in the morning of April 24, 1862, Farragut's main fleet started past the forts.

Before the Union ships were past, the moon rose and revealed them to watchers. Gunners at the fort hit Farragut's flagship, the USS *Hartford*. The burning ship ran aground on a sandbar right under Confederate guns. The crew put out the fire and backed the *Hartford* off the sandbar. Farragut continued north, leading eight big warships and several other gunboats.

The Union fleet then confronted the waiting Confederate fleet. Though weak and small, the southern fleet was eager to do battle. The ram *Manassas* did its best to strike Union ships, but it was too small to have much effect. As it headed back upstream, Farragut ordered the USS *Mississippi* to ram it. The *Manassas* was hit and set afire.

The Union fleet continued upstream and landed General Butler's troops. The city of New Orleans, knowing that it could not hold out, surrendered to Farragut.

Only Vicksburg, Mississippi, located high on a bluff over the river, was left to hold the eastern and western

Farragut's ship, the Hartford, *is seen at the center front in this view of the battle to take the forts protecting New Orleans.*

parts of the Confederacy together. Farragut decided that the navy would not be able to capture the city on the bluff, so he headed back to the Gulf of Mexico.

THE TAKING OF VICKSBURG

The Confederate navy was not finished. For many months, the CSS *Arkansas,* a ten-gun ironclad ram, had been under construction at Memphis. Before the Union army captured Memphis, the ship was hurriedly towed into the Yazoo River above Vicksburg, where construction was finished. The captain of the *Arkansas,* Isaac

THE HOAX AT VICKSBURG

In February 1863, the Union ram *Queen of the West* was under the command of Charles R. Ellet, son of the engineer who designed the rams. His job was to harass any Confederate shipping on the Red River in Louisiana and the Mississippi below Vicksburg. When Ellet accidentally grounded the *Queen* in the Red River, though, it had to be abandoned to the Confederates.

The southern navy quickly repaired the *Queen* and used it to chase after the *Indianola,* a big ironclad Union warship designed especially for use on rivers. The *Queen* and her accompanying gunboat managed to maneuver the *Indianola* into surrendering. As the Confederates took possession of the ship, however, the *Indianola* was grounded on a sandbar.

Furious at losing one of the best Union ships, Commodore Porter put his whole squadron to work building a fake ironclad on a barge. They then floated it downstream past the guns of Vicksburg. Rumors about the approaching ship spread until the Confederates, busy trying to refloat the *Indianola,* fled downstream to Port Hudson, Louisiana, near Baton Rouge. The men aboard the *Indianola* blew up all the weapons and abandoned her to the Union.

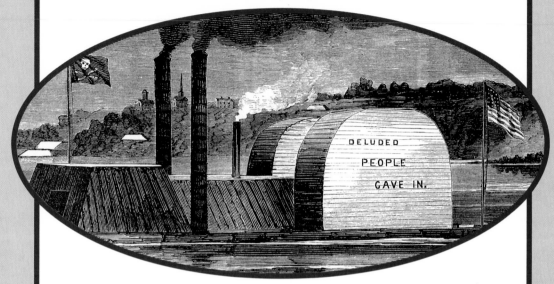

DELUDED
PEOPLE
GAVE IN.

Brown, sailed the ship back to Vicksburg in July 1862.

The entire Union river fleet, including Farragut's ships, sat at anchor near Vicksburg. The *Arkansas,* taking the Union by surprise, fired on the anchored ships. They could only return fire as the *Arkansas* chugged south, moving boldly past the larger vessels. Union fire bounced off the thick iron shielding, and the Arkansas got through and anchored at the foot of the bluffs of Vicksburg. A month later, the ship sank during an attack on the city of Baton Rouge, Louisiana.

For the rest of 1862, General Grant and Commodore Porter worked to capture Vicksburg. The river fleet alone

Admiral Porter's fleet of riverboats arrives at the levee to take possession of Vicksburg, last link in Union control of the Mississippi River.

could not capture the city, but it could keep the river open and carry General Grant's army troops into the area. Finally, Grant's men moved in to surround the city as Porter's gunboats bombarded it. The city's residents, cut off on all sides, took refuge in caves in the hillsides. After six weeks under siege, they finally gave up.

On July 4, 1863, Vicksburg surrendered, and thousands of Confederate troops were taken prisoner. The Union navy and army finally had complete control of the Mississippi River.

Chapter Five
Confederate Deep-Sea Raiders

Not all naval battles took place along the shores and rivers of the United States. Confederate vessels that managed to sneak past the Union blockade could also serve as warships on the high seas.

Immediately after the declaration of war, Confederate President Jefferson Davis put out a call to all shipowners in the South to make application for "letters of marque" issued by the Confederacy. These letters authorized private shipowners to arm their vessels and crews and to fight merchant and military vessels of the Union on the high seas. About twenty privately owned ships were fitted with these arms.

ESCAPING TO SEA

Commodore Raphael Semmes was convinced he could hurt the Union by attacking merchant ships. In 1861, he learned that the CSS *Sumter,* a small steamer docked in New Orleans, was available. Capable of making not more than 10 knots (11 mph, 17 kph), this vessel was not suitable for warfare. But that did not stop Semmes from converting it into a warship.

In just two months, the *Sumter* was remodeled and ready for sea. It set sail for Fort St. Philip and Fort Jackson, on the Mississippi just 20 miles (32 km) above the four passes to the Gulf of Mexico.

Semmes waited several weeks for just the right moment to strike. One night, the Union blockader USS *Brooklyn* was out chasing a would-be British blockade runner. Semmes ordered all hands to their stations and escaped through a pass into the Gulf of Mexico.

Almost immediately, the *Brooklyn* reversed course and began to chase the *Sumter.* Then a rain squall came up and its winds pulled the *Sumter* away. The *Brooklyn* gave up the chase. The first Confederate warship was free and ready for battle.

Semmes won his first battle against a 600-ton merchant ship, the *Golden Rocket,* off the coast of Cuba. The men stripped the big ship of all valuable equipment and set it afire. Semmes and the *Sumter* continued

Raphael Semmes (foreground) took the CSS Sumter *past the blockaders at New Orleans. After capturing nineteen Union merchant vessels, he was awarded command of the* Alabama. *He is shown leaning against a Dahlgren gun.*

across the Atlantic, scoring one victory after another. By the time they put in at Cadiz, Spain, in January 1862, Semmes had captured and burned nineteen U.S. merchant vessels.

The *Sumter* was badly in need of repairs, but the Spanish government refused to break its neutrality by letting it stay in port. They ordered Semmes to sea. He was given permission to sell the *Sumter* and head for England, where he was to take command of a much better ship that was under construction. Northerners were now cursing Semmes as a pirate on the high seas.

THE CSS ALABAMA

The ship intended for Semmes was a sleek vessel taking shape in an English shipyard. The Confederates would eventually name it the CSS *Alabama*. Although the builders claimed it was a merchant ship, everything about it indicated that it would be a warship. It was a propeller-driven steamer of more than a thousand tons, with two engines plus sail rigging. It was over 200 feet (61 m) long. With either sail or engines, the ship was capable of 15 knots (17 mph, 27 kph).

This impressive ship set out on July 28, 1862. It sailed to the Azores, a group of islands in the Atlantic Ocean, where the armament and final rigging were finished. The crew, except for a few officers, were British. The tug *Hercules* followed, carrying the cannon and ammunition that would be transferred to the new warship.

Coal and all other provisions were taken aboard the *Alabama*, and on August 24, 1862, it put out to sea again. It cruised the mid-Atlantic until it came upon the Union ship *Okmulgee,* a whaler from Massachusetts. Semmes captured the whaler without a fight, took what supplies he wanted, took the entire crew as prisoners, and set fire

The Alabama, *Raphael Semmes's pirate ship*

to the Union ship. In the next ten days, ten more ships fell to the *Alabama*.

Semmes continued into the South Atlantic. He tried the Pacific, too, but found few Union merchant vessels there. He returned to the Atlantic and put in at the port of Cherbourg, France, for repairs. The *Alabama* had been at sea for twenty-three months and had captured more than sixty Union vessels. The French, however, were strictly neutral about the U.S. war and would not permit the Confederate warship to stay.

A Union warship, the USS *Kearsarge,* was at sea just

Combat between the CSS Alabama *and the USS* Kearsarge

off the coast of France. Semmes sighted the *Kearsarge* and prepared the *Alabama* for battle. With its larger guns, the *Alabama* had a clear advantage. The crew and ship, though, were in bad shape after their 75,000-mile (120,000-km) voyage.

The skilled gunners aboard the *Kearsarge* shot huge holes in the *Alabama's* sides. The *Alabama* began to sink, and its engine fires were drowned. Semmes had no choice but to lower his flag and abandon ship.

Just as the ship was sinking, a British ship came by.

It picked up Semmes and some of his crew and took them to England. When Semmes returned to the Confederacy, the pirate-hero was promoted to the rank of rear admiral.

THE CSS SHENANDOAH

Soon after the *Alabama* sank in 1864, the Confederates bought another warship, which they named the *Shenandoah*. It set out for the Pacific under the command of Captain James Iredell. He was out of reach of communications when the war ended.

Iredell continued a very successful campaign of destroying almost all of the Union whaling fleet in Alaskan waters. He sank about thirty-five whalers in all. When he finally heard that the war was over, he sailed for England to surrender his ship. He refused to surrender to the Union.

THE FIRST
ATTACK SUBMARINE

The Confederate ship *H. L. Hunley* was the world's first successful attack submarine. Named after its inventor, it was a small craft—about 30 feet (9 m) long and only 4 feet (1.2 m) wide. It carried a crew of nine, eight of them providing power by manually turning the propeller while the captain served as the pilot. The submarine carried a single torpedo containing 90 pounds (41 kg) of gunpowder. After the *Hunley* rammed the torpedo against the side of an enemy vessel, a crew member lit a fuse to ignite the explosive powder and the craft quickly backed away. At least that was the way it was supposed to work.

Before the little submarine was ready for action, four trial runs were made. It sank every time. Thirty-two men, including the inventor, died in these attempts. Work continued, however, and on February 17, 1864, at Charleston, South Carolina, a brave new crew took the *Hunley* out of the harbor to attack a blockader. Its target was the USS *Housatonic,* a large, well-armed Union warship.

After darkness set in, the Hunley rammed its explosive charge into the *Housatonic.* A huge explosion blew a large hole in the Union warship, which sank immediately. So did the *Hunley.* The submarine was a victim of its own explosive charge. It was never found or rebuilt.

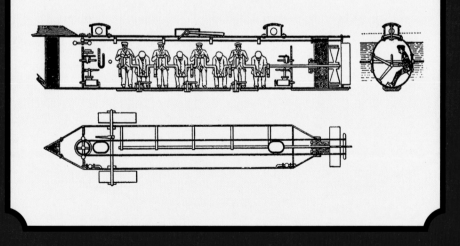

Chapter Six

"Damn the Torpedoes! Full Speed Ahead!"

In August 1864, Admiral David Farragut prepared to lead the Union navy in its final attack on the port of Mobile, Alabama. They would have to go through waters

The Union fleet entering Mobile Bay

infested with floating mines (called "torpedoes"). Farragut had wanted to attack the big harbor at Mobile back in 1862, after victories at New Orleans and on the Mississippi River, but the high command in Washington delayed this mission for two years.

Farragut finally convinced his superiors that danger to the Union fleet lay in the new Confederate ironclad ram, the CSS *Tennessee,* being built at Mobile. It was under the command of Franklin Buchanan, who had captained the *Merrimack.*

Mobile was vital to the South, so the Confederates kept it well protected. Fort Morgan, with its heavy guns, stood at the entrance to the channel approaching Mobile Bay. Fort Gaines and Fort Powell stood inside the bay. The Confederates blocked the entry to the bay with heavy pilings and mines.

THE UNION ATTACK

In early 1864, the Union agreed to furnish Farragut with ironclads and the necessary ground troops for an all-out attack on Mobile. Farragut's plan was to enter the harbor at high tide, moving at full speed with all guns blazing. Four ironclad monitors, *Tecumseh, Manhattan,*

ADMIRAL FARRAGUT

David Glasgow Farragut, born in Tennessee in 1801, was adopted after his mother's death by David Porter, a naval officer. Porter arranged for David to become a midshipman in the navy at age nine. He proved to be a whiz at naval affairs and was only twelve when he was given his first command.

Farragut was living in Virginia when the Civil War began, so Northerners questioned his loyalty to the Union. But this didn't stop Secretary of the Navy Welles from putting the sixty-year-old captain in charge of the West Gulf Blockading Squadron. His boldness in sneaking past the forts that protected New Orleans led directly to the capture of that important city in 1862. His loyalty was never questioned again. Farragut later wrote, "The passing of the forts was one of the most exciting sights and events I ever saw or expect to experience."

After his success at the Battle of Mobile Bay in 1864, Farragut was named the U.S. Navy's first rear admiral, the navy's highest rank.

Winnebago, and *Chickasaw,* would lead the way. They would direct their combined firepower of twelve big guns against Fort Morgan.

At dawn on August 6, 1864, the Union fleet of fourteen iron-reinforced ships began its advance. The lead monitor, *Tecumseh,* surged past Fort Morgan and was met by the *Tennessee.* Instead of following the original plan to stay close to land on the east, the *Tecumseh* swerved to the west, directly into a minefield. It struck one of the exploding devices, blew up, and sank.

The *Tennessee* suddenly slowed down and began to reverse. Its captain sighted the floating mines and was afraid they would destroy his ship, too. Farragut watched from the rigging of his ship, the *Hartford.* He realized that if his ships stopped, his entire fleet could be sunk by the eighty-nine guns of Fort Morgan, which had the boats in their sights. He ordered, "Damn the torpedoes! Full speed ahead!"

THE UNION FLEET IN THE HARBOR

Farragut's men could see the mines floating underwater just ahead. They held their breath as they felt the thud of mines striking the ship. But none exploded as they

MAURY'S MINES

Matthew Fontaine Maury, world-famous oceanographer, helped to develop underwater mines for the South. These mines, called torpedoes, floated just beneath the surface of the water and exploded when struck by a passing ship. They were especially useful in the defense of Richmond, Virginia. Mines sank or damaged more than forty Union ships during the last years of the war. The explosives, though, sometimes did not stay dry underwater. At the Battle of Mobile Bay, Admiral David Farragut was guessing the mines were waterlogged when he said his famous line, "Damn the torpedoes! Full speed ahead!"

sailed past Fort Morgan into Mobile Bay. They were now ready to confront the CSS *Tennessee,* under the command of Buchanan, and a fleet of three smaller wooden warships.

Two Union ships, *Monongahela* and *Lackawanna,* were Buchanan's first targets. His goal was to ram the Union ships, stop their advance, and keep them within range of Fort Morgan's guns. The Union vessels avoided his first attempt to ram them. Instead, they managed to ram the *Tennessee.* The Union fleet moved quickly into the harbor and out of range of Fort Morgan's guns.

The *Hartford* moved in and broadsided the *Tennessee.* As the battle went on, the *Tennessee* found itself alone—its three companion ships either sank or were out of the battle. Captain Buchanan was not about to give up, though, and he kept trying to ram his opponents, even though he was greatly outnumbered. After receiving heavy damage from continued Union gunfire, the *Tennessee* was forced to surrender. Buchanan was taken prisoner, and the Battle of Mobile Bay was over.

It had been a costly battle for the Union. Admiral Farragut called it "the most desperate battle I ever fought." But with the Mississippi River under Union

Gunners and officers worked together on Admiral Farragut's Hartford *during the Battle of Mobile Bay.*

control, with Charleston, South Carolina—the main Confederate port in the East—having fallen in February, and now with Mobile in Union hands as well, the South was completely blockaded. The war would not end for another eight months, but the South was trapped in its devastated land.

A FINAL NOTE

The Confederate navy grew from nothing at the start of the war into a substantial force. But it was never large enough or strong enough to take on the Union. If the South had started with a shipbuilding and repairing industry, like the North, its successes could have changed the outcome or at least drawn out the War Between the States.

At the time of the final surrender of the South in April 1865, the United States Navy had grown to more than 58,000 officers and men and 600 ships, including 60 ironclads. The United States Navy went on to become one of the greatest navies in the world.

MAJOR EVENTS OF THE CIVIL WAR

1860
December 20   South Carolina is the first southern state to secede from the Union.

1861
February 4   Representatives from the seceding states meet in Montgomery, Alabama, and form the Confederate States of America.

February 18   Jefferson Davis, previously U.S. Secretary of War, is inaugurated as president of the Confederate States.

April 12   War begins at 4:30 A.M. by a Confederate attack on Union-held Fort Sumter in South Carolina.

April 15   President Abraham Lincoln calls for 75,000 volunteers to help stop the war with the Confederacy.

April 19   Lincoln orders a naval blockade of southern seaports.

July 21   The First Battle of Bull Run (or Manassas) in Virginia is the first important battle; it is won by Confederate troops.

August 10   The Battle of Wilson's Creek in Missouri, another Confederate victory, brings lands west of the Mississippi into the war.

1862
February 16   The fall of Fort Donelson in Tennessee to General Ulysses S. Grant's Union troops opens up Nashville to capture; Nashville becomes the first southern city to be taken by the North.

March 9   The first battle of ironclad ships, the *Monitor* and the *Merrimack* (called the *Virginia* by the Confederacy), ends in a draw but revolutionizes naval warfare.

April 25   New Orleans, Louisiana, is captured by a fleet under the command of David Farragut.

September 4   General Robert E. Lee's Confederate troops move into Maryland, invading the North for the first time and heading toward Pennsylvania.

September 17   Lee's advance is stopped by the Battle of Antietam (or Sharpsburg) in Maryland, in the war's bloodiest day of fighting.

1863
January 1   The Emancipation Proclamation is signed, granting freedom to all slaves within the seceded states.

March 3   The U.S. Congress approves the conscription, or draft, of all able-bodied males between the ages of 20 and 45.

May	The first all–African-American regiment in the Union army, the 54th Massachusetts, begins serving.
June 3	Lee begins another advance into the North.
June 9	The Battle of Brandy Station in Virginia turns into the largest cavalry action of the War; the North is forced to retreat.
July 1–3	The Battle of Gettysburg in Pennsylvania ends Lee's attempt to take the North. From this time on, the Confederates fight a defensive battle within their own states.
July 4	The siege of Vicksburg, Mississippi, ends in a Union victory.
July 8	Port Hudson, Louisiana, surrenders, effectively cutting the Confederacy in half as the Union takes control of the entire Mississippi River.
July 13–16	Riots in New York City protesting the draft kill or injure hundreds.
November 19	President Lincoln delivers the Gettysburg Address as a dedication of the national cemetery at Gettysburg, Pennsylvania.

1864

March 10	General Grant is put in charge of the entire U.S. Army.
August 5	The Battle of Mobile Bay in Alabama is won by the Union fleet under Admiral Farragut.
September 1	The Union army, under General William T. Sherman, captures Atlanta, Georgia.
October 19	After more than two months of fighting in the Shenandoah Valley of Virginia, General Philip Sheridan's cavalry regiments take the valley in the Battle of Cedar Creek, leaving the Confederates without an important source of food or a place to regroup.
November	General Sherman's army marches the 300 miles (483 km) from Atlanta to the Atlantic Ocean, living off the land and destroying everything the Confederates might find useful.

1865

March 13	Out of desperation, the Confederate Congress votes to recruit African-American soldiers. Five days later, the Confederate Congress no longer exists.
April 2	Richmond, Virginia, the capital of the Confederacy, falls to the Union.
April 9	Lee surrenders to Grant at Appomatox Court House in Virginia.
April 14	Abraham Lincoln is shot by southern sympathizer John Wilkes Booth. He dies the next day.
December 18	The Thirteenth Amendment to the Constitution, abolishing slavery, goes into effect.

FOR MORE INFORMATION

FOR FURTHER READING

Hakim, Joy. *War, Terrible War.* A History of US, Book Six. New York: Oxford University Press, 1994.

Durwood, Thomas A., et al. *The History of the Civil War.* 10 vols. New York: Silver Burdett, 1990.

Tracey, Patrick. *Military Leaders of the Civil War.* American Profiles series. New York: Facts on File, 1993.

VIDEOS

The Civil War. 9 vols. Produced by Ken Burns. PBS Home Video.
The Civil War. 2 vols. Pied Piper.

CD-ROMS

African-American History—Slavery to Civil Rights. Queue.
American Heritage Civil War CD. Simon & Schuster Interactive.
Civil War: Two Views CD. Clearvue.
Civil War—America's Epic Struggle. 2 CD set. Multi-Educator.

INTERNET SITES

Due to the changeable nature of the Internet, sites appear and disappear very quickly. The resources listed below offered useful information on the Civil War at the time of publication. Internet addresses must be entered with capital and lowercase letters exactly as they appear.

The Yahoo directory of the World Wide Web is an excellent place to find Internet sites on any topic. The directory is located at:
http://www.yahoo.com

The Internet has hundreds of sites with information about the Civil War. The United States Civil War Center at Louisiana State University maintains a Web site for the gathering and sharing of information:
http://www.cwc.lsu.edu

The Civil War in Miniature by R. L. Curry is a collection of documented facts and interesting tidbits that brings many of the different facets of the Civil War together:
http://serve.aeneas.net/ais/civwamin/

The National Park Service maintains sites on hundreds of Civil War battles. The directory of these sites is at:
http://www.cv.nps.gov/abpp/battles/camp.html

One site specifically on the Battle of Mobile Bay is at:
http://www.mnf.mobile.al.us/area_history/battle.html

The Hunley Web Site contains information on the CSS *H. L. Hunley* submarine, such as where and when it sank, how the bodies were recovered, and how the torpedo worked
http://members.aol.com/litespdcom/index.html

INDEX

About the Author

Wallace B. Black was a pilot flying in India and China during World War II. Having lived history, he became fascinated by it. He is the author of a twenty-book series for young people about World War II. Building on his lifelong interest in the American Civil War and the West, he and his wife, Jean F. Blashfield, developed the American Civil War series for Franklin Watts, but he was able to write only two of the books before being sidelined by ill health.

Mr. Black graduated from the University of Illinois, played the saxophone in various wartime jazz bands, and worked in children's publishing all his life. He was the creator of many books and encyclopedias now found in schools and libraries.